The 'ow' Cow
VI

By Viola & Zaida Stefano

VeeZee Publications

Copyright © VeeZee Publications Pty. Ltd. 2024
First published in Australia in 2024
by VeeZee Publications Pty. Ltd.
veezeepublications.com

The right of Viola Stefano to be identified as the author of this work have been asserted by her in accordance with the **Copyright Amendment (Moral Rights) Act 2000.**

All rights reserved. Apart from any use as permitted by the author & under the **Copyright Act 1968**, no part may be reproduced, copied, scanned, stored in a retrieval system, recorded, or shared, by any means or in any form, without prior written & signed authorization from the publisher.

ISBN: 978-1-923120-07-5

A catalogue record of this book is available from the **National Library of Australia.**

Author: Viola Stefano
Illustrations, cover & internal designs: Zaida Stefano

Illustrations copyright © Zaida Stefano 2024
Design copyright © Zaida Stefano 2024

Disclaimer: The content presented in this book is meant for educational purposes only. The author & publisher claim no accountability to any entity or person for any liability, damage, or loss caused or assumed to be caused directly or indirectly as a consequence of the application, use, or interpretation of the material in this book.

Core words used in this book

I	want	**can**	stop	**look**
like	more	he	go	**see**
here	what	do	**the**	**and**
out	where	we	it	**up**
not	they	when	**that**	**down**
she	**now**	them	**is**	put
help	off	you	yes	on
turn	who	this	no	why
done	make	**a**	to	under
come	**in**	some	which	**there**
open	get	good	same	home

Look! The cow is here in the cool, blue pool.

The cow looks up and sees the owl.

The owl looks down and sees the cow.

The cow looks left now
and sees the fowl.

The fowl looks right and sees that cow.

The cow looks up there now and sees a sow.

The sow looks down and can see that cow.

The sow looks up and can see the owl.

The owl looks down and can see the sow.

The cow looks up there now and can see ranger Brown.

Ranger Brown can see the cow, fowl, sow and owl.

cow	fowl	owl
Brown	sow	now
	down	

We hope you had fun reading!

Learning made easy with VeeZee

VeeZee Publications

Wait, there's more!

Visit our website for information about our range of readers & supporting products.

veezeepublications.com

www.ingramcontent.com/pod-product-compliance
Lightning Source LLC
Chambersburg PA
CBHW042107090526
44590CB00004B/128